THE ENGLISH
GENTLEMAN IS DEAD

Long live the English Gentleman!

For John Major

THE ENGLISH GENTLEMAN IS DEAD

Long live the English Gentleman!

DOUGLAS SUTHERLAND

Illustrated by
TIMOTHY JACQUES

CANONGATE

First published in Great Britain
in 1992 by Canongate Press Plc
14 Frederick Street, Edinburgh, EH2 2HB

Copyright © Douglas Sutherland
Illustrations © Timothy Jaques
ISBN 0 86241 401 6

British Library Cataloguing-in-Publication Data
A catalogue record for this book is available
on request from the British Library

Printed and bound by Biddles Ltd, Guildford

CONTENTS

One People, One Country, One Leader, One Class

Preface

On the 9th April, the day following the General Election of 1992, The English Gentleman was formally declared to have died. In his hour of triumph Prime Minister John Major announced that his long-promised classless society was about to become a reality. It was something which caused a sharp intake of breath in homes great and small up and down the country as the nation contemplated this latest threat to their established life style. Of all Mr Major's election promises, the creation of a classless society is the one of which the nation most stands in dread.

To claim that the British are the most class-conscious people in the world is untrue – that is a distinction which belongs to genuine democracies like the United States of America – but the traditions of a class-dominated society go deep. They reach back to the arrival in Britain of the Romans fifty-five years before the birth of Christ and were given another sharp shot in the arm when the Normans arrived from the French side of the English Channel in 1066.

To comprehend the full enormity of Mr Major's declaration this breathtaking proposition should be put in its correct prospective. By comparison, the promise of the Labour Party, if elected, to abolish the use of all titles and to sweep away the House of Lords pales into insignificance. The whole basis of society in Britain depends upon whether one is a gentleman or not and has nothing whatsoever to do with titles. To quote such authorities on the matter as Sir James Lawrence in his

1

book *On the Nobility of the English Gentry*, published in 1834:

'Gentility is superior to nobility; nobility may be acquired; gentility must be innate.' Or of his contemporary Seldon in his *Titles of Honour*.

'A king might ennoble a man by giving him his coat of arms ... but he would no more have thought of creating him a gentleman than of creating him a giant.'

It is true that in modern times the whole question has become blurred at the edges and has degenerated into nit-picking about class. Some four years ago an American Professor, Paul Fussell, published what turned out to be a runaway bestseller in the U.S.A. in which he declared all Americans to be divided into no less than nine grades of social status. The categories started with top-out-of-sight which was reserved for the very richest of the rich and finished up with bottom-out-of-sight which was one degree below financial destitution.

We have not yet arrived at quite this degree of refinement on this side of the pond although there is some evidence that the day may not be far off. At a recent Royal Garden Party on the lawns of Buckingham Palace, one elegantly dressed lady was heard to put down another, equally elegantly turned out, with the words: 'My dear, I would remind you that my family have been *nouveau riche* for a great deal longer than yours have!'

Such fine distinctions in fact beggar the whole question. In England to be a gentleman is to be the top of the social tree. They have always regarded themselves as inheriting the earth and, by and large, that is a belief they still hold.

When, rather more than ten years ago, I published a series of slim volumes in which I sought to describe the species, I freely admitted that I might be describing one which was on the verge of extinction. In this I have proved to be quite wrong. The English Gentleman is alive and flourishing. He has merely changed his spots.

In the pages which follow I describe him in his new habitat and point to the caste marks by which he can be distinguished in his new guise for the guidance of the earnest student in the not-so-gentle art of social climbing in our new classless society.

Douglas Sutherland,
Offémont, Oise.
Easter 1992

The Army meant a life of leisure

Jobs for the Boys

Perhaps the most striking thing about the New English Gentleman is that he has lost, or rather voluntarily abdicated, his amateur status. The age-old tradition by which the eldest son inherited all the trappings of gentility including not only the family lands but, more importantly, all the money, still remains where there are any lands or money to succeed to. The equally time-honoured tradition by which younger sons went into the army or the Church has now been totally relaxed.

This has proved to be no hardship for younger sons. The days when to serve in a good regiment in the army meant a life of gentlemanly leisure, devoted entirely to such sports as polo and pig-sticking, interrupted only by such highlights as leading the Charge of the Light Brigade, relieving Lucknow or winning VCs at the Massacre of Rorke's Drift, are now over. The modern high-tech army with its insistence on the most vigorous Commando-style training in times of peace, culminating with pressing a button to destroy a distant enemy in times of war, are not at all to his taste.

By the same token the life of a Churchman has lost much of its charm. No longer can the country parson rely on five days hunting a week and preaching a sermon on Sundays or being automatic choice as Captain of the village cricket team. Today the term 'muscular Christianity' has been taken far too far in the opinion of all but a few.

On the other hand, there are now many other avenues open to younger sons in which it is no longer considered disreputable to earn a living.

Even elder sons have taken on a new lease of life in these democratic days. It is not any longer the case of his being restricted merely to chasing foxes on horseback or keeping down the pheasant population. It is now open to him and, indeed, often obligatory for financial reasons, for him to take on the tilling of his own lands. This is described as being a 'gentleman farmer' as opposed to being a farm labourer and this is something that many elder sons find much to their taste. It means that they can now drive their own tractors around with their caps worn at a distinctive angle as well as assisting in mucking out the cowsheds in their green wellies. All capital good fun.

It is the younger sons, however, who are more and more finding that the world is their oyster. It is not in any way to their detriment to remark that the jobs in which they find themselves happiest are not generally of a cerebal nature. Professions such as the law, medicine or school teaching are best left, as they always have been, to the brighter sons and daughters of the middle classes.

There was a time not so very long ago when it became quite a fashion to join the police, especially when this entailed pounding the beat in Mayfair or the neighbouring square mile of vice, Soho. At one stage there was at least one heir to a Dukedom and several sons of Peers of the Realm who were so employed, but of late this particular occupation seems to have lost some of its appeal. Perhaps this has something to do with having to spend so much of their time booking friends who have overstayed their welcome on parking meters instead of chasing dangerous criminals, which would have been much more to their liking.

Another popular diversion was working the buses either as conductors or, more excitingly, drivers. This has not altogether lost its charm, but it seems to have passed its peak. At its height the more fashionable routes like the Number Eleven which passes along the King's Road in Chelsea was monopolised almost entirely by Old Etonians. That these particular buses were known for their practice of travelling together, nose to tail, with long gaps between each convoy, was put down to the spirit of the Eton Boating Song 'We'll all row together'. Driving a bus, at least in one instance, has not proved to be a dead-end job. One Peer of the Realm, whilst so employed, was talent-spotted by the illustrious publishing house of Debrett's Peerage and promoted straight onto their Board of Directors to advise them on matter relating to the aristocracy, a field of knowledge in which they had found themselves temporarily short-handed.

Lorry-driving is another, rather similar, field which has found appeal, largely because it offers greater scope for individuality than is possible when wearing the uniform which is required of personnel on buses. Not only can the gentleman lorry driver dress exactly as he chooses but he can indulge himself in such things as, for example, taking his sporting dogs along with him as travelling companions. Thus it is no unusual sight for travellers up and down the motorways to see a couple of labradors lasciviating from the driver's cab with probably a few fox terriers joining in the chorus. Lorry-driving also provides the opportunity for the driver to call in on any of his friends who happen to live near his route, although not all owners of stately homes are overjoyed to have an

Travelling companions

eight-wheeler come sweeping up their avenues.

It might be thought that, for members of what are often described as the privileged classes, to take jobs such as these shows at best a lack of initiative and at worst as taking the bread out of the mouths of the much more deserving. This is to misunderstand totally both the nature of the species and the situation in which they find themselves in a changed world. Among those from less secure social backgrounds, to pound a policeman's beat or drive a bus might be considered as letting down the aspirations of their parents who have sacrificed so much to let them have a better chance in life. Nothing could be further from the truth of the matter. Most upper-class families have quite enough to do looking to the fortifications of their own privileged lives to bother about such trivialities.

If they were to think about it at all, it would be simply in the light of how lucky they are. In their day they would have been going through a traditional phase described as 'sowing their wild oats'. This usually amounted only to throwing bread rolls and being sick in the champagne bucket at debutante parties or being arrested for knocking off policeman's helmets on Boat Race night, but it is now rightly considered as a less acceptable alternative to a safe job on the buses.

Besides which, there are many other directions which the careers of young gentlemen can take today which are viewed by their elders with much greater suspicion. One of the more sinister of these is doing what is mysteriously described as 'Something in the City'.

In former times this was very much more clear cut. Sons of middle class families would go off to become stockbrokers or to sell insurance or even to join banks at which, it was hoped, they would make a great deal of money and so get a leg-up in the world. This is no longer the case. It is now all something to do with computers. After the last war there was a vague description of an activity with faintly disreputable overtones, known as being in 'export-import'. This was followed by property dealing and more recently, and equally vaguely, something called public relations. All of these have now been dwarfed by the dawn of the age of the computer.

The effect of the arrival of the computer in the City and elsewhere is not, however, vague at all. It has meant that, whereas in more staid times it was expected of anyone seeking a career in the mysterious world of high finance to serve a long and arduous apprenticeship before any spurs could be earned, today instant fortunes can be earned by even the most inexperienced at the touch of a button. Or, perhaps to be more fair, long hours spent gazing at a small television screen and pressing lots of buttons.

The strain of this instant fortune-producing activity is such that its young practitioners become addicted to a wild and disorderly lifestyle, fuelled apparently by the intake of vast quantities of, of all things, lager beer. The next stage in their progress is marked by the acquisition of designer clothes, improbably fast motor cars and, the ultimate accolade, a house with an L-shaped drawing room somewhere in Chelsea or South Kensington.

This is the sort of fate against which the upper classes, not always with complete success, but understandably try to warn their children.

Caste Marks

The wind of change which has resulted from the upheaval of those whom I have, for want of a better description, generically described as gentlemen as opposed to non-gentlemen, has not just blown up out of a clear blue sky. Nor has it anything to do with Mr Major's decision that all distinctions of class are to be abolished forthwith.

The pulling-up of the roots of what is essentially a country-dwelling species to be replanted in a different environment has been going on for quite some time and was greatly accelerated by the 1939-45 war. There was a time when one gentleman passing another in the street whom he did not know would immediately recognise a fellow member of the species as surely as Stanley recognised Livingstone. It was something to do with what naval gentlemen used to describe as 'the cut of one's jib'. It is in fact all to do with what might be described as caste marks and these, like what it meant by 'the cut of one's jib', are becoming increasingly difficult to define.

At the end of the nineteenth century the difference between a gentleman of quality and lesser mortals was as wide as an ocean. It was considered that a family could not rise from the ranks, as it were, to being socially accepted in under three generations. Today we live in an age of instant gentlemen. The caste marks, however, still exist and the aspirant to acceptance as a gentleman ignores them at his peril. Nor is it possible to list the essential ingredients after the manner of a cooking recipe, like having clean fingernails, hold-

11

I can't help having a caste mark

ing your knife and fork in the approved manner or getting up when a lady comes into the room.

In essence it all boils down to a matter of self-confidence. As I have remarked in another place, a Gentleman believes in God because by and large he is confident that God believes in him. It is remarkable what an assumption of this sort can do for a fellow in his passage through life and in his dealings with his fellow men. The foundations of this self-confidence are traditionally laid during the upbringing of the embryo gentlemen by the life-style of his forebears, later to be beaten into him at a suitable educational establishment.

The blurring at the edges of the caste marks thus acquired is certainly in part due to the number of young gentlemen of impeccable background who have revolted, in these more liberal times, against the system. How, for example, is one to know that the youth in an open-necked shirt, with his hair done up in a pony tail, picking his nose in the corner at a formal party is the eldest son of a Marquess? This is not, however, an example that the candidate for promotion to social honours would be advised to emulate. For them the unwritten rules should be closely adhered to.

The way to the upper reaches of the social mountain is an arduous one and there have been a number of cruel trip-wires set across the paths of the unwary, both male and female, since Miss Nancy Mitford published in the 1950's her guide to what was U and non-U in upper-class speech. Before you could say 'Gor Blimey!', eager matrons from Pinner to Crouch End were rabbiting on about "Looking Glass, Looking Glass on the Wall. Who is the Fairest of us all?" and converting their cosy little mantelshelves into baronial chimney pieces.

The wickedest jest of all was when Mr Peter York and the ingenious Miss Ann Barr invented a wonderful tribe which they called Sloane Rangers because, it was said, they proliferated in the no-man's land around Sloane Square which lies somewhere between Chelsea and Belgravia. The girls sported headscarves by Gucci and Janet Reger knickers and took their Range Rovers to go shopping in Harrods, whilst their male counterparts commuted to the City in Barbour waterproof jackets and green Wellington boots. Before you could say knife, the upwardly mobile were all at it, anxious to be seen to identify with that they imagined to be one step further up the social mountain whilst the establishment looked on with what can only be described as gleeful amusement.

The invention of the Sloane Rangers was a leg-pull where the victims never saw the joke. The fissure into which they fell proved altogether too deep for them ever to climb out of again. Latest reports say that they are breeding down there and that there are tiny Sloane Rangers running around all over the place.

It may be that there are false crests which still abound for the dedicated social climber but equally it is true to say that at no time in our history has it been easier to gain acceptance in that most desirable of worlds, the charmed circle of the English Gentleman.

So while all that is required is to develop the confidence, remember, it is still an act of foolhardiness to jump out of the airplane without first checking the parachute straps.

The upwardly mobile were all at it

"Packed the wrong bag"

Dressing the Part

In the second half of the 20th century it is true that the English Gentleman has had to shed something of his country image and assume the trappings of an urban life. This does not, however, mean that the way he dresses has become any less distinctive than it has always been; a style which is envied and imitated throughout the world.

I have related elsewhere the story of the gentleman who encountered a friend walking along Piccadilly who remonstrated with him on the way in which he was dressed. 'Nobody knows me in London,' the gentleman protested, 'so how I dress does not matter. In the country everybody knows me, so it does not matter there either.' Although there is a certain logic in this philosophy, it does not in fact do the English Gentleman justice.

Certainly a gentleman would never dress for effect but this does not mean that it is not something which he feels to be beneath his notice to devote any thought. He would no more think of disregarding the advice of his tailor when having a suit made ('built' is the correct expression) than he would instruct his surgeon on how to remove his right leg should such an operation become necessary. He is essentially a conventionalist.

What gentlemen seek to avoid at all costs in their dress is any suggestion of the sort of flamboyance which might be calculated to frighten the horses. In short, gentlemen in their appearance never seek to *glitter*. Such wardrobe items as designer shirts and underwear or other ostentatious adornments have no place in his life.

MIND OVER MATTER

It might be helpful to observe that the way a gentleman dresses has nothing to do with his financial circumstances. The tweed jacket with leather patches on the elbows, which is so often thought of as his hallmark, is not an affectation. It is usually simply a case of his not being able to afford a new one. To have leather patches sewn on or cuffs relined without there being any necessity is one of the worst forms of affectation.

By the same token it is unlikely that he would have in his wardrobe anything which he would call a sports jacket. This is simply an in-built mental attitude more than anything else. A gentleman will often have a great number of jackets but each will have a specific purpose. Thus he will have a jacket in which he goes shooting which is called a shooting jacket and when this becomes too old and disreputable looking, it will be demoted to the role of a gardening jacket. He will probably have a blazer or two inherited from his cricketing or rowing days or simply to lounge around in when he is not required to wear a suit, just as he will have a hunting jacket to go hunting in or a dinner jacket for when he goes out to dinner. It goes without saying that he will wear the appropriate trousers for each occasion. I only mention this about trousers because, when recently I enquired about hiring a dinner jacket from a dress hire firm, whose name I shall not discredit, the assistant enquired whether I would require the trousers as well. Of course, when putting on a dinner jacket you will need to put on the appropriate trousers as well. It is just that this is never referred to as a dinner suit. In the same way the words 'black tie' or 'white tie'

18

on an invitation to a formal occasion does not mean that this is the only article of dress you are required to wear. There are, however, certain small details, particularly when wearing formal clothes, to which the social aspirant would do well to pay attention.

The wearing of one of those made-up bow ties which clip on round the back of the neck is a practice which is very much frowned upon. One might suppose that this is a form of snobbery as it indicates that the clothes have been hired for the occasion just like those dreadful waistcoats which come with a hired morning coat with only elastic straps to hold them together at the back. In fact there is not nowadays any snobbery about hiring clothes for formal occasions. It is just an objection to mixing with a lot of people dressed like waiters. He is a wise man who indulges in the modest investment of his own morning waistcoat even if he cannot afford the whole suit, and to acquire the skill of tying a bow tie is not an onerous one. It is also advisable when hiring morning clothes not to rely on the inevitable 'morning' tie the dress hire firm will thrust upon you. It is becoming more and more the practice to wear an old school tie with these clothes. In fact, to wear an old school tie on other than formal occasions is increasingly considered to be bad taste. This is something I shall refer to again when it comes to looking at the whole public school business.

This attention to detail is also reflected in the number of cuff buttons on a gentleman's suit. It is the sort of triviality on which it is wise to be careful. Traditionally only bespoke suits sport four buttons on each cuff. The others have only three. As part of

The number of cuff buttons on a gentleman's suit

the very high cost of a handmade suit, a customer can expect that all the button holes are handsewn and all the buttons sewn on to last a lifetime. A button which comes off in the first ten years of a suit's life would, in the view of the more old-fashioned customer, justify its being sent back for free servicing. Most important is that cuff buttons should unbutton so that, among other things, a gentleman can turn them back when he is going through the ceremonial washing of hands. For cuff buttons to be sewn on to a suit purely for show is regarded by many to be as bad as the wearing of a made-up bow tie or keeping their trousers up with a belt instead of braces.

Of all the details which go to make up the way a gentleman dresses, perhaps the most important of all concerns the head and the feet. Generally speaking, a gentleman always wears well-polished leather shoes. The traditional high polish of a gentleman's footwear derives from the days when every gentleman had his own personal servant either as a batman when in the army or a valet in his private life and for whom the most exacting chore was the task of keeping his master's riding boots and other footwear up to snuff. In these servantless days it is still considered to be rather *infra dig* for a chap to be seen to be cleaning his own shoes. However, in households where chivalry has not yet died, there are quite a few gentlemen who draw the line at deputing the task to their wives and anyway it is something that many wives are not awfully good at. This is an example of one area in this modern world where some gentlemen are having to bite the bullet for the sake of keeping up appearances and do the job for themselves.

What a gentleman wears on his head is another matter for debate in a world where everything is changing. It is basically true that, ever since the wearing of morning clothes with the then obligatory top hat whenever he came up to London went out of fashion, the gentleman has dispensed with a town hat. There was a brief period when gentlemen coming up to London to see their men of business like lawyers or bankers favoured the bowler or, as it is more correctly described, the Coke (pronounced Cook) hat as a compromise with the more formal topper. The Coke hat had originally been designed as a hard hat which could be worn when out hunting on less formal days. When it became adopted by businessmen for City wear, however, it dropped out of fashion with their country cousins. In these days when so many gentlemen have become urbanized most of them now go bareheaded about their daily business. By contrast, to wear a hat for any open-air activity in the country is almost universal. However, whatever the occasion, it is not the hat the gentleman chooses to wear but the way that he wears it that makes him distinctive.

Perhaps there is no hat in the whole repertoire which demonstrates this better than the common or garden flat at which the late Norman Wisdom made so much the hallmark of the working man. Where the pigeon fancier from Birmingham and all points north wears his cloth cap with the brim pointing defiantly outwards and upwards, the gent somehow manages to wear it tipped down over his forehead so that the brim runs more or less parallel with his nose. This in turn means that if the wearer is to see where he is going he has to tilt his head

If the wearer is to see where he is going

back and gaze on his fellow men with a look of disdain akin to a guardsman on parade. It is something which takes quite a lot of practice. I believe this is the origin of the expression 'to look down your nose' at people. The gentleman does not really mean it. It is just one of his many curiosities.

The overall look common to all gentlemen, which has its origins in his nursery days, is of being well-brushed and well-scrubbed. The only difference in his more mature years is that, as the day goes on, he stays that way longer.

Fashions change in these matters but, in the present day, most gentleman are clean-shaven. In fact beards, apart from a few naval officers and arctic explorers, have been out since the days of Edward VII. The day of the well-clipped moustache in the military style once so much the fashion is also now very much out since its universal adoption by the more rampant homosexuals. Only in the way the hair is cut is there now a certain amount of lassitude. Where the short-back-and-sides-look was once more or less *de rigueur,* many gentlemen now wear their hair much longer, even to the extent of the pony-tail look not always being confined to young gentlemen's sisters. The more conventional, however, are usually content to display their individuality by allowing the hair a certain amount of length at the sides and brushed up into the sort of quiffs which used to be known as 'bugger's grips'. The origin of this expression is now lost in antiquity which is perhaps just as well.

Bugger's Grips

The Gentleman and his School

It had always been the practice for the upper classes to send their sons away to school during the most formative years of their lives, which means from the age of about seven until at least seventeen. The school year is divided into three terms – Spring, Summer and Winter – with breaks at home in between to recover. (At Eton for some reason they call these terms 'halves' but then arithmetic has never been a very strong subject for Etonians.)

This is what is known as having a public school education and is the cause of much resentment among those who consider that it gives the privileged classes an unfair advantage in life, as well as causing some confusion, particularly among Americans, who would call it having a private education.

It is not within the scope of this learned work to speculate on the advantages or disadvantages of a public school education other, perhaps, than to remark that it is those who seem to envy its opportunities most who are the most fervent advocates for its abolition. This is something with which quite a few of those experiencing its rigours might well agree. What does, however, concern us here is the role of the public school in a classless society. Like much else this has changed almost out of recognition in recent years.

The original idea for parents digging into their pockets to send their sons, and in some cases their daughters, away to boarding schools was not merely for the excellent reason of getting them out from under their feet. It was also that they should learn the truth about the cruel world into which they had been born at as early an age as possible. That public schools were commonly believed to be hotbeds of homosexual depravity, savage corporal assault and worse did not weigh heavily with parents determined that their offspring were to be given every advantage in an unfair world.

It is only natural that the more left-wing educationalists who advocate with such shrillness the levelling down of all educational standards so that the thickest should not feel themselves to be inferior, should also seek to instruct the less fortunate in what they feel to be the more desirable aspects of the public school educational system. Some of the most advanced thinkers in London's State schools are now adding professional instruction in the delights of homosexual activities to the curriculum to make sure that their pupils do not miss out on what they consider to be an unfair advantage enjoyed by the children of rich parents who can afford to send them to boarding schools for what they fondly believe to be the same purpose. In short, this whole public school business is now threatening to get totally out of hand.

The remedy lies very largely in the hands of the social-climbing classes to seek to impress on anyone who will listen just what top-notchers they are. It is in the worst possible taste, for example, to bring in the name of the educational establishment which your offspring adorn on every possible and impossible occasion. Some parents seem to be in a state of perpetual motion. 'We are just taking/collecting/visiting little Willie to/from Winchester/Rugby/Millfield, etc. He's at school there, you know', is in the same category of vulgarity as, 'I just sent round for my Rolls/BMW/Bentley', when

27

speaking to somebody who is hard pushed to afford a bicycle. Equally revealing is the habit their offspring have acquired of naming establishments they attended. They too never just went to school but to Private/Boarding/Public school. Such qualified descriptions are not part of a gentleman's vocabulary.

This pretentiousness is the same sort of thing as flourishing the old school tie on anything but formal occasions or, perhaps even worse, sporting a blazer with a badge emblazoned on the pocket. There are a few exceptions to this generality about blazers such as those stage-comedian type jackets affected by rowing buffs at Henley Regatta, rather after the fashion of a fancy dress party, but on the whole, school memorabilia is best consigned to the closet in afterlife.

The public schools themselves have now almost universally bent the knee to accommodate the whims and aspirations of their new social climbing clientele in a classless society. They are no longer the grimly monastic establishments whose views on the correct education for young gentlemen have gone unchallenged for generations. Not only have they largely abandoned the use of the lash to maintain proper discipline but have actively condoned parental interference in the educational process by encouraging unlimited visits, exeat weekends for pupils, special occasions, treats and unlimited telephone calls. In less indulgent days visits were limited to taking the little beasts out for one afternoon at half-term and telephone calls were only resorted to at times of serious illness or death.

Now, to crown everything, the public schools have opened their doors to girls. Why it should be

"And that one's for lunch in the Steward's Enclosure."

considered that girls, who hitherto have had their own perfectly adequate colleges, should now be thought to gain from moving in with a lot of spotty boys, is unclear. Come to that, why is there no reverse traffic with boys being admitted to such schools as Roedean or Cheltenham Ladies College? Can it be something to do with parents not wishing to deny their children the advantages of a comprehensive school education?

Even in what can be described as either the good old days or the bad old days, according to opinion, the question of which establishment was to be favoured with the responsibility of educating one's children was very much a matter of horses for courses. In many cases it was a matter of son following father, in others of geographical convenience, but also, and probably in the majority of cases, the current reputation of the schools concerned. Like almost any other enterprise, schools, and public schools in particular, have their ups and downs, largely dependent on the virtues or the vices of the headmaster, in much the same way as the reputation of public houses vary with the esteem in which the landlord is held.

Eton, by tradition, is viewed as the most prestigious of all schools and the one which gives its alumni the greatest, and therefore the most unfair, advantage in later life. This has nothing to do with the commonly held belief that the Battle of Waterloo was won on its playing fields but because it was believed to be the most expensive and that everyone who went there had to be out of the top social drawer. Much to the irritation of Old Harrovians, their school was generally considered to come only second, with the rest nowhere. This is nothing to do with the excellence or otherwise of the various academies of learning but rather with the quality of the parents which they attract. By this standard Eton has dropped quite a bit in recent years in the league ratings. There is now a general feeling among the more conservative that to send a boy there smacks of the show-off, not to say of the *nouveau riche*. Harrow has held its place better, perhaps on account of having kept a lower profile.

Gordonstoun, which has always been a frightful show-off school ever since Prince Philip went there, with their banging-on about being such a spartan seminary, has never been much cop with the establishment. Certainly in recent years, in common with Harrow, it has enjoyed favour with some of the mega-rich oil sheiks, but this, by general consensus of opinion, is not the same thing. Similar reservations are held about some other of the less historic foundations like Millfield whose enormous fees, one is tempted to conjecture, can only appeal to those parents for whom its main attraction is that it demonstrates their ability to pay them.

Schools which come highest in the public schools league today are the solid schools of sterling worth, with Winchester, largely reserved for the very brainy, coming somewhere near the top and with Marlborough, Rugby and Repton not far behind. Mention too must be made of the top Scottish schools like Glenalmond, Fettes and Loretto which seem to attract far more pupils from south of the Border than before.

Whatever the answer to all these questions may be, it would be wise for prospective parents to study the form book with care before placing their bets.

The Gentleman and his Club

In exactly the same way that the traditional public schools have shifted their place in our increasingly class-conscious society, so too has the English Gentleman's Club.

In an earlier work on the English gentleman (Debrett's Peerage, 1978) I recounted two incidents at that time which bear repetition if only because they illustrate the habits and prejudice of clubs and clubmen in those days which now seem so long ago.

The first was a conversation which took place in my own club between two of the older members and which concerned the merits or demerits of a new member who had just been elected.

'To tell you the truth,' remarked one old buffer to the other, 'I think that fellow is a bit of a bounder.'

'I'll go further than that,' said the other. 'The fellow is a liar.'

These were strong words indeed. To be a bounder was one thing but to be dubbed a liar was quite another. However, the proposer of this slander proceeded to produce the strongest possible evidence.

'The fellow told me he had a house in the country but I've found out that he lives in Surrey!'

The second was an incident which was reported to have taken place in one of London's most august clubs which numbered more dukes amongst its membership than any other.

One morning one of the most ducal of the dukes, in a state of great agitation, summoned the secretary of the club to the front hallway.

'D'ye know what has just happened?' he boomed, when the secretary, who must be all things to all members, arrived. 'I was standing here minding me own business when this fellow I have never seen in me life before came up and bid me good morning.'

'Oh dear,' said the Secretary. 'What did you do, your grace?'

'Well,' said the Duke, reasonably enough, 'I didn't want to appear rude so I just turned me back and walked away.'

Although this story is probably apocryphal it does illustrate the truth, as it then was, that a gentleman did not join a club to be clubbable. He joined for all sorts of other reasons. It was somewhere where you could have purchases sent to avoid being seen carrying a parcel in the street; because you did not have to tip the club servants; or simply because your father had been a member before you.

In Regency days the clubs of St James's were, of course, very clubbable places indeed where like-minded spirits met to drink and gamble the nights away. Even in Victorian times and after, the great soot-blackened palaces which lined Pall Mall had quite a substantial number of members who dined regularly in their clubs but this dwindled away to a trickle after the last war. There always remained, however, the tradition that a gentleman ought to be a member of a decent club. He put the name of his club without any address on his visiting card and only scribbled his home telephone number on the back if he wanted to see the person again. Clubs remained not very friendly places.

All that has now totally changed. It started, like many another revolution, in a small way. Rather tentatively, a few of the clubs which were particularly strapped for cash converted over-large washrooms or other surplus accommodation into annexes where members could invite their wives to dine if they were not inclined to take them out to a decent restaurant, and from this unspectacular beginning the revolution grew until it took on the proportions of a flood.

Today there are very few clubs indeed, even in the first league, which do not encourage lady guests and even, in extreme cases, allow ladies associate membership. Such delicacies as rice pudding and treacle tart, once the culinary triumphs of any decent club, have in many cases disappeared from the menu altogether and the older members are driven to sulk in remote corners of the silence room whilst the once sombre halls are filled with the sound of popping champagne corks and the tinkle of girlish laughter.

All of which is not at all a bad thing. Nor is it to say that the English Gentleman has altogether taken flight at this growing invasion of less well-entrenched members of the establishment who are apt to slap each other on the back in an excess of bonhomie and some of whom may even have houses in Surrey.

It is still certainly a 'good thing' for the aspiring gentleman to seek the membership of a decent club and to aim to send his children to an acceptable educational establishment. It should only be remarked that the attainment of these two laudable ambitions does not necessarily signal his social arrival or perhaps not to the same extent as

The tinkle of girlish laughter

before the establishment of a classless society. It does however pose the conundrum of which club one should join.

There are certain clubs which are automatically ruled out on grounds of ineligibility as, for example, the Service Clubs to which membership is only open to officers who have served in the armed forces. Chief among these is what used to be the Cavalry Club before it amalgamated with the Guards and which in turn brought about a new lease of life for both. They now share splendid premises in Piccadilly, looking across Green Park to Buckingham Palace, with sometimes painful memories of ceremonial parades. Also along Piccadilly is the Naval and Military, known to all as the 'In and Out' because of the traffic directions printed in large letters on their gateposts, while down in St James's Square is the Army and Navy, invariably known as 'The Rag', for reasons at which even Mr Brewer will do no more than hazard a guess.

Then there are the clubs whose membership is drawn from what are loosely known as the Arts. There are a surprising number of these, with the Garrick named at the top of the pile and with the longest waiting list. Only recently did this chauvinistically male club avoid what some would have thought to be its inevitable fate – opening doors to lady members.

Easier to join and rather more matey is the Savile in Brook Street, Mayfair, and down a notch or two are the Arts Club in Dover Street which admits members engaged in advertising and the once very jolly Savage. Some years back the formation of a new arty club, mainly for writers and publishers, called Groucho's, was founded in Soho by a determined group of feminists in the publishing business who had become greatly piqued at being excluded from the chauvinistically male portals of the Garrick. It seems to have enjoyed a sort of *succes de scandale* and now has a waiting list of its very own.

One of the Clubs which has dropped off the end of the ladder is the delightfully shabby Chelsea Arts Club, once the home from home of many distinguished but usually impecunious artists. Threatened with financial oblivion, it was taken over to be run on a more commercial basis and is now reborn as the haunt of a *soi-disant* 'Chelsea Set' who appear to be a hybrid form of Sloane Ranger and young men who are 'something in the City'. The survivors among the older members venture there nervously, fearful that, should they wish to cash a cheque, something so innovative as a banker's card should be demanded of them.

GENERAL LIST

Almost every club founded in the Victorian era set out to provide for a specific membership, even if the definition was as vague as that of the Travellers' Club whose membership qualification demanded of the candidate that he should have travelled one hundred miles, measured in a straight line, from London. Of clubs formed only for the purposes of social intercourse by and large only those of the Regency survive, where once Regency Bucks spent their nights of dissolution in drink and gambling. Alas today White's, Boodle's and Brooks's, all in St James's Street, are rather duller dogs and have assumed an exclusivity which is almost impregnable. There are, however, several 'good clubs' whose fortifications are easier to breach.

There is, for example, the Royal Automobile Club with quite the grandest premises in Pall Mall, and a Country Club outside London to boot, where the qualifications for membership are simply that one should be a motorist. Inevitably dubbed 'The Chauffeur's Arms' by the irreverent, it certainly boasts the finest recreation facilities in London. It has a swimming bath where Cabinet Ministers and their wives frolic, squash courts, sauna baths and all the other keep-fit necessities for the desk-bound city businessman.

At the other end of Pall Mall is a rather more august establishment, the Athenaeum, a palace of marbled-hall magnificence, whose membership tends towards the spiritual rather than the temporal. It is said that the late Lord Birkenhead used to make a habit of stopping off there on the way from his town house to the House of Lords in order to relieve himself. On being remonstrated with by a member of the propriety of this as His Lordship was not himself a member, Birkenhead replied: 'Good God! Is this place a club as well?' Today there are so many bishops who are members that the Athenaeum has earned for itself the nickname of 'The Clergyman's Rest'.

Another club which has tended to open its doors rather wider of late is the Turf in Carlton House Terrace. As its name implies, this provides a watering-hole for the racing fraternity. It is now, however, not obligatory to own a string of racehorses, although there are still many members who do.

Also changing its spots of late is the aforementioned Travellers' Club from which Phineas Fogg set out on his epic journey *Round the World in Eighty*

"I'm afraid you've been blackballed, sir."

Days. It was a Club much favoured by officials of the Foreign Office down the road in Whitehall which was perhaps why top spy Sir Anthony Blunt found it such a congenial haunt. Donald Maclean was also a member, whilst Guy Burgess, his running mate in the Spy Stakes, used the Reform Club just down the road. Clubland has always been a happy hunting-ground for spies. Whether by accident or tacit agreement, high-ranking members of MI5 and MI6 tend to hold themselves aloof from such goings-on behind the jealously guarded doors of White's Club.

So there it is. You pay your money and take your choice – providing, that is, that the club may choose to have you as a member. There still remains, even in these egalitarian times, the ever-present threat of the blackball as the fate of the aspiring member whose face, it is decided, does not fit, despite the recommendation of his proposer and seconder.

The Gentleman at Home

How are the domestic habits of the English Gentleman bearing up in a changing world? The traditional habitat of the species is in over-large houses,
hidden behind high walls in the depth of the
countryside and as far removed from London as
possible. Many are still there. When, in his poem,
'Granchester', Rupert Brooke wrote: 'Oft between
the boughs is seen the sly shade of a Rural Dean',
he could as easily have been writing of the English
Gentleman today. They keep low profiles, as they
always have done, going quietly about the business
of keeping down the game on their estates whilst
their wives continue to preside over the Girl Guides
and open the village flower show or sales of work.

There are many, however, who have found
themselves, in the changing economic climate,
unable to continue to afford this isolation, even
after ruthlessly dispensing with the services of the
domestic staff once considered essential to their
modest comfort and, reluctantly, keeping a closer
eye on their wine merchant's bills.

Some have simply moved to smaller houses and
let their former mausoleums to businesses or insti-
tutions of one sort or another or, better still, sold
them to pop stars or others of equal ambition. It
has not come easily to them. Gentlemen, for many
perfectly sound reasons, require much more
lebensraum than ordinary people. One gentleman,
on being congratulated by a friend on the comfort
of a newly-acquired residence exploded, 'Good
God, man! I haven't even got a gunroom.'

There are even some who - such are the de-

41

mands of their new status in the ranks of the gainfully employed - have moved to London and such places. These are usually among the youngest and most adaptable of the gentlemanly classes and it quite often leads to their losing their distinctive caste marks so that they become indistinguishable from the herd. However, most continue to preserve the distinctive characteristics of their upbringing and background. For the benefit of the serious student of the habits of the English Gentleman, it might be helpful to note here some of the more important of these.

DOGS ABOUT TOWN

Gentlemen are never really happy without a dog or two around the place. However, they are the first to recognize that their normal companions in the countryside, like labradors or spaniels, are totally unsuited to town life. Nor would they ever consider the acquisition of any of the larger breeds of non-sporting dogs which have become so much the status symbols of the less socially secure such as Alsatians or Dobermann pinschers or, in extreme cases, of the clearly inferior Pit Bull Terriers.

The solution lies in keeping one or other of the smaller breeds of lap dog, much given to yapping and messing up the furniture. As most gentlemen have been brought up to despise such breeds and their owners, they go about getting them in a rather sneaky way. They let it be known to their wives that they would not object to her keeping, say, a Pekinese or a Dachshund or two for company whilst the breadwinner is about his daily business. This comes with a lot of propaganda to demonstrate what an understanding kind of chap he is,

42

"...And was it a lovely party, dear?"

not to mention how self-sacrificing.

No sooner has the pooch arrived than the gentleman takes complete charge. It is he who not only supervises the diet but serves it its food personally. If he does not actually admit it to the matrimonial bed (most do), he goes to great expense to provide it with luxurious sleeping quarters, rubber bones and enough cuddly toys as would satisfy the most indulged of children. He will even take it 'walkies' every night and put a ban on any of the local pubs which do not admit dogs.

The first dog usually proves to be only the thin end of the wedge. With one animal established in the household the population tends to multiply despite all protests of the gentleman's wife that she never wanted a dog in the first place and that they are driving her round the twist.

ACCEPTABLE DOGS
The King Charles Spaniel is probably the top dog for top people. They are affectionate creatures with a surprising ability to moult all the year round. This does not affect the gentleman as he is not a brush-and-pan man, leaving this to the better-equipped mother figure.

Others in the running are the aforesaid Pekinese and dachshunds, pugs, chihuahuas and perhaps Jack Russell terriers who generally confine their snapping to only the youngest children. Corgis are the most ungentlemanly of all small dogs, having appalling house manners and biting anything without discrimination. Maybe that is why Her Majesty The Queen keeps so many around her.

ENTERTAINING AT HOME
Much agonizing is currently going on among am-

bitious hostesses about the niceties of entertaining in the home. Just how cosy should that informal little dinner party be or just how grand the show-off affair designed to impress the impressionable with one's *savoir faire* and, by coincidence, with one's financial and social standing which so many nowadays seem to regard as one and the same thing? The more socially confident rely on the old and tried formula of good food and excellent drink.

FORMAL OR INFORMAL

This small volume does not pretend to be any sort of guide to etiquette and modern manners. That is something which is best left to the great authorities on such things who are constantly volunteering advice on arcane matters such as how to address a Bishop's wife or ten things you can do with a finger-bowl.

One of the most debated topics is what clothes should be worn when invited to dinner. To change or not to change? That is the question. The answer is, of course, that one should *always* change if invited to dine, even if it amounts only to putting on a clean shirt or changing one's knickers.

A gentleman coming in from a day striding over his broad acres would certainly not contemplate sitting down to dine, with or without company, smelling of the farmyard. For the city dinner guest to do so smelling of money or whatever he has been fiddling with all day would be equally inappropriate. It is only a question of what you change into. The hostess who says, 'Just come as you are', does not really mean it. Equally the guest, determined to show just how laid-back he is, should not turn up in jeans, open-neck shirts and jogging shoes.

...Things you can do with a fingerbowl

At the other end of the scale there has recently been an outburst of allegedly private dinner parties, with the guests, all in full fig, posing with sophisticated unconcern, which somehow appear amongst the glossy pages of society magazines as a testimonial to the 'cleverness' of the hostess and the scintillating company she keeps. This is a far cry indeed from gentlemanly behaviour and can only be put down to the desperate struggles of the socially-determined to claw a place for themselves in the sun.

TO COME BEARING GIFTS

There is a growing practice amongst those invited to dine at someone else's house to bring with them a gift, usually in the shape of a bottle of wine. This is, although no doubt most kindly meant, in fact the height of bad manners. There is always the suggestion that the bearer has only done so for selfish reasons to try and ensure that his host does not run out of the stuff, or, alternatively, as a criticism of the quality of the host's cellar. This, in turn, raises the question of the quality of the wine brought. To bring a cheap bottle of plonk is surely something of an insult but to bring a splendid chateau-bottled vintage can be taken as the most heavy-handed hint of what the guest expects his host to produce by way of matching it.

There are, of course, bottle-parties where the guests are under an obligation to come accompanied by one or more bottles. On these occasions the question of quality control can also be tricky. I remember one host who gave a very grand bottle party every year. He adopted the practice, when guests arrived, of having them check in with their invitation cards for the laudable reason of foiling gate-crashers but at the same time gave instructions that whatever they had brought be carefully noted against each guest's name. This so irritated one guest that, when attending the party the following year, he had a bottle of Air-Wick registered against his name.

The only generally accepted obligation of a guest when asked to dine is that he should return the compliment, should the opportunity offer, of asking the hosts back.

TO WRITE OR NOT TO WRITE

Despite my determination not to trespass on the territory of the etiquette experts, I feel that a brief note on the subject of 'thankyou' letters might not come amiss. The reason is that although what are known as bread-and-butter letters are the very essence of gentlemanliness and their importance is beaten into the very young almost before they have left the nursery, the whole thing is now being carried far too far.

To write a letter thanking your hostess for having you to a cocktail party (drinks party nowadays *Ed*) is an example of this. After such an occasion the women present ring each other up anyway to discuss who did what to whom. If you don't know you hostess well enough to indulge in this enjoyable exercise, it is the height of sycophancy to write. The same thing applies to a dinner, or, even more so, luncheon party. The only excuse for writing under these circumstances is if you have left something behind which you want forwarding, or the name of a fellow guest which has escaped you, but this is much more easily done on the telephone. If, however, you want to apologise for being sick in the champagne bucket, or some similar misdemeanor, a letter is certainly called for and, incidentally, the easiest way out.

A letter is only obligatory if you have been to stay for a night or more. A useful piece of advice on these occasions is always to mention the house dogs by name or even make them co-addressees. This is guaranteed to endear you as an appreciative guest and is far more important than remembering the names of the children.

A GOOD ADDRESS

In the days when all the grander aristocratic families had their town houses to complement their landed estates and which they only occupied in what was then known as The Season, their location was a matter of the greatest importance, reflecting as it did the standing and social importance of the families concerned. The square mile of Mayfair and, to a lesser extent, Belgravia, were greatly in favour on account of the proximity it gave their mansions to Buckingham Palace where they were required to attend many Court functions. Those were the days when to live in a house which was just a number in a street was socially impossible. You either lived in a Grosvenor House, a Dorchester House or houses with names like Crewe or Apsley or Londonderry or you really did not exist at all.

It was the 1914-18 war which put the hat on all that. Mayfair, after a spell as the playground for the upper classes, for a time became the dormitory for a greater concentration of prostitutes than any other capital in Europe. It has now fallen into the hands of advertising agencies, property dealers and gambling clubs, whilst Belgravia has been given over to Embassies or houses converted into flats for Americans and mega-rich business men.

Unfortunately the commercialisation of former areas of desirable housing for the gentry has now spread far beyond the bounds of Mayfair and Belgravia. Chelsea, once the home to impecunious artists and not a few solid middle-class citizens, has now been swallowed up, as has that once genteel area of Kensington where once all families of any standing supported a maiden aunt or two living in gracious if reduced circumstances.

Today the leafy glades of Kensington Gardens, where once uniformed nannies pushed babies in crested prams, are the haunt of balding business-men, perspiring heavily as they jog furiously by in their immodestly short pants and gym shoes which are now for some obscure reason described as 'trainers'.

So where now in London are the newly-urbanized gentry finding refuge? Basically they have been driven over the frontier into what was once no-man's-land. Disraeli, speaking in the House of Commons, once declared, 'I would send Her Majesty's Forces to discover and conquer new, uncharted land, were it not that I know none, except the other end of the Cromwell Road.' That is now a boarding house area almost exclusively colonised by Australians so the nearest area in which gentlemen can find refuge is presently at the other end of the Fulham Road where they buy neat little cottage-type houses and can usually find a space to park their Land Rovers.

The next most popular area of conquest is south of the Thames in areas like Battersea and

As they jog ...

even Clapham Common, pronounced 'Cla-am' by the socially self-conscious. In fact it is not far removed from John Major's own childhood stamping-ground of Brixton. Whatever can things be coming to?

There used to be a saying that you should never hunt a fox or commit adultery south of the Thames. I suppose quite a long time has passed since a fox was killed on Clapham Common but it is now quite a normal sight to see tweedy couples striding across the Common with a pack of dogs in tow, metaphorically thrashing themselves to death with a riding crop. About the other bit, I have no first hand information.

Battersea is a rather different proposition, tending to be inhabited by the not-quite-so-confident in social terms who seek to identify with an earlier conceit and describe themselves as living in South Chelsea. This causes a certain amount of tittering in the bushes of Battersea Park.

There are one or two other areas in London where gentlemanly communes are seeking to establish a toehold. Hampstead, delightfully countrified though it has always remained, and where foxes are a positive pest, has for too long been the preserve of left-wing, *soi-disant* intellectuals. Besides which the Heath, if accounts by the media are to be believed, is made hideous at night with the strident cries of homosexuals on the rampage. Buggery is not yet accepted in the English Gentleman's glossary as an approved blood sport. Nearby Primrose Hill has shown greater promise, and even parts of Highbury and Islington, but only time will show whether or not the species is likely to become indigenous.

The Gentleman Abroad

In the days when the English Channel was the English Channel and the only way to get abroad was to cross it in a boat, it was generally considered by us British to be a stretch of water provided by Providence to insulate us from the necessity to fraternise with foreigners.

In this connection it is perhaps worth noting that when William the Conqueror made his one-way crossing with his band of mercenaries in 1066, none of them showed the slightest desire to return to the badlands of Normandy. It was a case of *j'y suis, j'y reste*, and that is the way it remained until not so very long ago.

In fact, in 1939 there were only two paddle steamers plying between Dover and Calais. I can well remember, at a rather grand diplomatic occasion in the 1930s, overhearing a delightful snatch of conversation between an elderly lady of obviously Teutonic origins, and a true blue-blooded Englishman. Evidently the lady had not circulated in society long enough to recognise the species for she was heard to ask earnestly:

'For how long haff you in Engeland been?'

'Madam,' said the English Gentleman, drawing himself up to his full height and looking down his patrician nose, 'my family came over with William the Conqueror.'

'Ah,' said the lady sadly. 'What a pity are we are missing each other. We came over with the *Maid of Kent*.'"

Dear me! How all that has changed now. To look at one of those maps which chart the cross-channel ferries is almost as confusing and bewildering as to try tracing the shunting yards at Crewe. Add to this the Armada of airplanes which roar daily out of Gatwick, Heathrow and all places North for all places South, each heading for the most recently developed Blackpool-sur-Mer and it will be realized that things are not quite what they used to be. Now, to crown it all, we have started to tunnel underneath it. May the Lord preserve us.

Even the description 'abroad' as it applies to holiday-makers today no longer means, as it used to do, a little paddling in the not-so-blue waters of the Mediterranean or sliding down Swiss mountainsides on planks of wood. When you read in the report of a society wedding that 'the honeymoon is being spent abroad' you can bet all the tea in China that the happy couple will be winging off to some faraway tropical island, squashed together with all those competitors in television quiz shows who have won 'the holiday of a lifetime'.

This changing scene is something with which the English Gentleman is finding it very difficult to come to terms. I have remarked in another place that the English Gentleman did not, traditionally, go abroad very much except to fight a war or help build an empire. It has also been said, with some justice, that it was the English Gentleman who invented 'abroad' from the holiday-maker's point of view. These two contradictory statements are in fact quite easily reconciled.

There was a time, reaching far back in our island history, when members of the aristocracy attended by retinues of hangers-on in the disguise of tutors or companions went on Grand Tours, taking in centres of culture like Italy and Greece and some, like Lord Byron, got quite a taste for abroad. It was not, however, until Victorian times that gentlemen took to going abroad out of the shooting season and in search of pleasure. The leader of the pleasure hunters was, of course, the Prince of Wales, afterwards Edward VII, after whom a legion of squares, boulevards, streets and hotels were named by the French, grateful for his efforts in promoting tourism among the upper classes. Where the Prince led, many followed in the belief that in places like Paris, ladies divested themselves of their clothing more readily than at home (untrue) whilst such unlikely candidates as the first Lord Brougham, after serving as Lord Chancellor of England, retired to the South of France to spend the second half of his long life popularising Mediterranean seaside resorts like Cannes and Nice.

The point about going abroad for gentlemen in those days was to *do* something like hunting boar in the Ardennes, taking the waters at spas all over Europe for their livers or teaching the Swiss the delights of sliding down their own mountains. Upper class families never went on the bucket-and-spade type of holidays enjoyed by middle class families when the breadwinner got his annual break from the treadmill. To a certain extent this is still true, but, now that many sons of gentlemen and even gentlemen themselves have been forced by circumstances to become gainfully employed with all the restrictions of freedom that that implies, it may be worth looking at how they are coping with the effects of social upheaval.

It is still certainly true to say that the average English Gentlemen does not go abroad simply to do nothing and sit on a beach. Nor does he alto-

The gentleman does not go abroad simply to do nothing

gether trust hotels, and the middle class passion for time-share holiday homes has completely passed him by. Chalet parties in the more fashionable ski resorts and dancing the nights away with the international set has no very great appeal. If he wants to go ski-ing – and quite a few do – he will seek somewhere remote and is perfectly happy whooping it up with the locals.

As most English Gentlemen have been brought up in the country where to enjoy blood sports is pretty well obligatory, if the spirit moves him to go abroad or if he is bullied into it by his wife, it seems a sensible compromise to go somewhere where he can kill something. Shooting wild boar in the Ardennes is very much an in-thing to do. So is partridge shooting in Spain or salmon fishing in Norway.

Many gentlemen who still own their estates but are forced by economic pressure to let their fishing and shooting to foreigners are not so downcast about this as they might have been before they became more tolerant of 'abroad'. Now many of them, gleefully stuffing the loot in their back pockets, head off to all manner of exotic places like Iceland and Alaska where they can often get better sport for less money.

There are even reports that some of them have gone off to tropical paradises like the West Indies where they immediately hire a boat and set out to sea in search of big game fish. Anything to get away from those damned beaches strewn with naked bodies smothered in sun-tan oil.

"Ah - zat ees no ordinary fly - zat ees Anabolia Nervosa or Brown Sedge, Sir."

Eating Out

It has been said that you can immediately tell a gentleman from a non-gentleman the moment he sits down at the table. There is some truth in this and it perhaps applies even more when he is not in his own home but entertaining or being entertained in a restaurant or other public place.

This not only concerns the way in which he holds his knife and fork, although it is certainly true that the upper classes handle their cutlery in quite a different way from the rest. Quite why this should be I cannot imagine but to do it the 'wrong' way is not to get off to a very good start. Do not, for example, hold you knife as if it were a pencil.

It is also very important to get the vocabulary right. This is something that even wine and food writers seem to get wrong and is perpetuated by whoever writes the menus in less than top class restaurants.

For example there is really no such thing as a first course called 'starters'. 'What would you like to start with?' is a perfectly reasonable question put by a host who wants to know the wishes of his guests. 'What will you have for starters?', with the suggestion that everyone is lined up on the starting line waiting for the gun to go off before racing through the menu is a modernism which is just about as gauche as the word 'afters' when referring to the pudding course.

Another strange exercise in semantics, which I believe to be an important Americanism, is the practice of referring to the head waiter as the 'maître d'. 'Maître d' what I am not quite sure. Nor am I sure whether it is supposed to indicate that the user of the term is a sophisticated multi-lingual man-of-the-world or simply an attempt at 'talking posh'. Whichever it may be it is all part of showing off and, of all the deadly sins against gentlemanly behaviour, showing off is the deadliest sin of all. In no field of endeavour is the social mountaineer more likely to fall into a crevasse than over the dinner table. Here are some of the pitfalls.

ORDERING THE WINE

In our classless society there are two skills to which none who strive to stand out from the common herd will ever admit to being less than an expert. One is in driving a motor car; the other is to being something of a connoisseur of wine. It only requires of the wine waiter to offer the wine list for inspection to bring on an attack of all the worst symptoms of winemanship in the amateur. He will settle down to go through it page by page, pursing his lips and rubbing the side of his nose with his forefinger as if trying to make up his mind whether to bid for the *Mona Lisa* or Holbein's *Madonna*. But this is as nothing to the palaver which takes place when the wine of his choice is finally brought to the table. He will sniff it suspiciously, hold it up to the light and sip it, rolling it round the tongue with an oscillatory action painful to watch before giving a gracious nod of approval or the thumbs-down treatment.

All of this is a rather pathetic performance when all the wine waiter is doing in pouring a few drops into the host's glass before serving it to his guests is asking him to judge whether it is corked or not – 'corky' in the wine boffin's dictionary. All

"Ees OK - I getta da Fire Breegad!"

that is required of him is to give the wine a quick sniff and a brief nod to the waiter. The more extreme histrionics indulged in by the shower-off are the subject of the most acute embarrassment to his more knowledgeable guests and wine waiters frequently have to retire to conceal their mirth.

THE GREAT CIGAR RITUAL

The choosing of an after-dinner cigar can be another opportunity for the over-enthusiastic host. Really the only decision to be arrived at when the cigars are displayed is what size you want, but this is often not good enough for Flash Harry. He will pick them up in turn, sniff at them (surprise! surprise! they smell of tobacco), hold them up to his ear to see if they crackle which they usually will unless they are soaking wet and examine the brand name on the band with all the concentration of a watchmaker fitting a new hairspring.

There is a generally-held but erroneous belief that the band on a cigar should always be removed before lighting the thing. Not to do so is considered a social solecism practised by bookmakers who do not know any better. To bookmakers should be added discerning gentleman who always light a cigar with the band on. To do otherwise is to risk damaging the outer leaf which can destroy the whole thing. The cigar will shrink slightly after it is well alight when the band can be removed much more easily if wished. This arcane piece of information can be used with great effect to put down the less knowledgeable.

ORDERING THE FOOD

It is a normal and quite harmless conceit for the better restaurants to print their *cartes* in *français*.

This custom springs from the belief that all the best chefs are French and their *specialités de la maison* can only be described in their *langue d'origine*. This does not really present any difficulty as most people know their *boeuf* from their *poisson* and can imagine the rest or ask the waiter. It is perfectly permissible for the diner to discuss such matters in French but only if he has a reasonable command of the language. Otherwise this constitutes showing-off and will almost inevitably lead to being shown up. A knowledge of foreign languages is anyway considered rather suspect in gentlemanly circles.

This is something which is even more danger-ous when ordering the wine by name; when the Montrachet comes out as the Mon-trashy. It is safer and better to order the chosen wine by its number on the list to avoid disappointment.

TIPPING

A dangerous area, this. It is generally said that it is vulgar and ostentatious to overtip. The suspicion that this is put about by the parsimonious under the excuse that it is ungentlemanly is probably very well-founded. A gentleman is just as capable of taking a sneaky advantage over another party as anyone else and will overtip shamelessly if it means having his glass filled up more regularly than the next man. It is shrewdness rather that showing-off to overtip the doorman of grand hotels. It means that you will be greeted with extra deference when next you arrive and ensure that you are the most likely to be found a taxi when it is raining.

MANNERS

It is said of the gentleman that he is never uninten-tionally rude, which is a very different matter from

63

being never rude at all. Nowhere is this more evident than in his relationship with those who serve him. An example of this is the use or omission of the prefix 'Mister'. To address someone by surname only is not a slight. It is a compliment reserved for; (a) his schoolfellows or those of his own class whom he does not know intimately but of whom he approves; (b) those more humble beings who are concerned with his personal comfort and whom he holds in high esteem. This includes not only his personal servants but waiters, barmen, doormen and perhaps his barber whom he promotes to the same degree of intimacy as if he was on his own staff. The only people to whom he applies the prefix 'Mister' are those whom he wishes to keep at arm's length, like Government officials, tradesmen to whom he owes money, politicians with whose politics he does not agree, or his bank manager. By the same token, a gentleman, in common with Americans, is always at pains to get a person's name right when he is introduced to them socially unless he has reason to dislike them - in which case he gets the name deliberately wrong. Thus Mr Smith becomes Mr Jones, Mr White becomes Mr Black and Mr Bottomleigh becomes Mr Bumley.

It should also be noted that gentlemen are always scrupulous in the matter of titles. No matter how well he may know a Peer of the Realm he will always refer to him formally when mentioning his name to a third party who does not. This is in sharp contrast to the name-dropper who tries to impress his friends with his intimacy with well-known people by using their first names whether he knows them or not.

Bloodsports

The impression generally given of the *modus viv-endi* of the average English Gentleman is of a man who, on getting up in the morning, goes over to the window to draw the curtains and remarks, 'What a perfectly lovely day! I must go out and kill something.'

This is not an absolutely accurate picture, but it does draw attention to an aspect of the life style of the English Gentleman which those aspiring to the description try most assiduously to emulate. It has resulted in a great upsurge of would-be gentlemen throwing aside their city suits and heading for the hills with the back of their Range Rovers stacked with an assortment of guns, rods, dogs and other impedimenta, even including the occasional wife or dolly bird.

At the same time, since, in a classless society, a man must be all things to all men, he will make a substantial donation to the Green Party written on re-cycled paper, rather as real gentlemen make an annual donation to the Royal Society for the Protection of Birds before the pheasant shooting season starts.

One of the more deplorable aspects of this back-to-nature movement which is so rapidly becoming an epidemic in our classless society is the determination with which its apostles seek to introduce their new-found faith into their, and everyone else's, lives. It cannot be long before businessmen start bringing home their work in game bags instead of brief cases and their wives turn up to church in green wellies.

"Duck!"

MIND YOUR P's AND Q's

As with most things, there are a number of pitfalls into which the over-enthusiastic can fall. One of these is a tendency to get the correct terminology ever so slightly wrong. For example there is the impulse to refer to all game birds in the singular. This is right most of the time as, for some reason, many game birds, like grouse, duck, snipe or wood-cock, do not have a plural. However, birds like the pheasant and the partridge do have a plural. So whilst it is grammatically correct to announce that you are to go pheasant or partridge shooting, you actually set out to shoot pheasants and partridges. It grates dreadfully on the ear for somebody to say that they are going to shoot pheasant, partridge or, for that matter, pigeon or rabbit or anything else that has a plural.

This is a similar solecism as talking about a billiard-room instead of a billiards-room as the place where you go to play a game called billiards, not billiard. However, the semantics of the shoot-ing field or the river bank are dwarfed by compari-son with those of the hunting field, or, for that matter, among the sailing fraternity, where they can't even call a rope a rope but must call it a sheet.

TALLY-HO

One of the chief targets of our classless society is the hunting of foxes, regarded as the most unac-ceptable blood sport of all, so it might be worth looking a little more closely at what this is all about.

The main reason for someone trying to stop someone else from doing anything is, as often as not, motivated by one of the more deadly of the Seven Deadly Sins, envy. Thus the campaign to

67

stop the privilege of an expensive education or shooting a grouse hurtling down a heather-clad hillside or catching a salmon alongside the royal family on the royal Dee is apt to be dog-in-the-manger stuff and seldom for the reasons of high idealism under which the anti-everythings like to fly their banners.

At the same time it must be said that not all of those who go hunting do so out of a burning mission in life to keep down foxes for the sake of the farmer's chickens. There is the story told of one Master of Foxhounds who had occasion repeatedly to reprimand an over-enthusiastic follower for acts of indiscipline. Finally, in exasperation, he demanded, 'What the devil do you come out hunting for anyway?' To which the wretch replied that he supposed it was for the fresh air and exercise. 'In that case,' snapped the Master, 'why don't you just go home and bugger yourself with a pair of bellows.'

Others are unavowedly there for the social life, it being a generally held belief that you meet people at a higher level when seated on a horse and, by all accounts, a hunt in the bushes in the early hours of the morning at the end of a Hunt Ball would be to discover a great deal of Tally Ho! in progress. As one old rustic, leaning on a gate chewing a straw remarked to another as the hunt streamed past in all its glory, 'Sex maniacs, the lot of them!'

It is often envy of this privileged life-style which gets up the noses of the down-with-foxhunting fraternity rather than a deep well of sympathy for the fox. At the same time the opportunity it offers them for punch-ups at hunt meets up and down

"Are they chicken or chickens?"

the country does make a nice change from other rent-a-mob activities, which are usually in towns. This is not to say that many non-country dwellers do have a very real, if sentimental, aversion to blood sports.

All in all, to take up hunting does not do a great deal nowadays for the aspirations to join the ranks of the gentry, as might be generally imagined. But then it was never really supposed to.

MIND YOUR MANNERS

By contrast there are certain aspects of the head-long rush of the lemmings to embrace the traditionally gentlemanly sport of shooting which can easily turn the whole business into a positive social disaster.

It has always been considered among gentlemen that the great thing in shooting is to weigh the odds as heavily as possible in favour of the game. This is in sharp contrast to the sporting instincts of the fisherman who is capable of pulling any scurvy trick on a fish in an effort to get it to swallow his worm.

There was a time when the quality of a shoot was judged between gentlemen by how difficult it was made to hit the birds. Every inducement was offered, for example, to persuade pheasants to fly as high and as fast as possible over the guns and so maximise their chances of living to a ripe old age. Not any more so.

The trouble lies with the adoption by big business of shooting as the ultimate in what is called Corporate Entertainment for the sake of public relations. For this purpose they take a fine shoot, arm all their customers, and set out to shoot as many birds as possible in the allotted time. In these circumstances it would not be a contradiction in terms to provide fast, high birds, but their efforts in the opposite direction cause rather more than a snort of anger or contempt amongst members of the establishment.

In certain extreme cases the new sporting gentry demand that the pheasants which have been specially reared for the occasion should be driven over the guns straight out of their breeding pens which means that, if they can be induced to struggle into the air, they come over so low as to be in danger of knocking your hat off.

This can prove a double-edged weapon. It is nowadays quite a normal arrangement to pay for a day or two's shooting according to the number of dead birds picked up. There was a recently reported occasion where the dead bird arrangement was in operation which caused much hilarity. It was a two-day shoot and the guests were having a high old time as the pheasants rained out of the sky and the total of the bag rose inexorably. Finally, on the afternoon of the second day, the Company Secretary, who had been hiding in the bushes with an adding machine, could stand it no longer. Breaking cover, and at great danger to life and limb, he threw himself in front of the guns, waving his arms in the air and crying 'Stop! Stop!' He had just worked out that one more drive and the Company would have to go into liquidation.

In fact the whole shooting scene is beginning to look like reverting to the bad old days of the Edwardian shooting parties where hosts plunged themselves into bankruptcy to provide bigger and bigger bags for the edification of the Prince of

"They say you meet people at a higher level"

Wales and his cronies and the number of the birds killed counted for everything. But then the Prince and his entourage were not gentlemen either.

DRESSING THE PART

Just as it is as well to get the vocabulary right, it is important to dress the part as to the manner born if it is hoped to cut any ice socially. The first thing to remember is not to overdo it. To turn up at a shoot or on the river bank dressed like a Christmas tree and hung around with every possible gadget is to risk ridicule and have the head keeper or the river ghillie back away nervously.

Fishermen are particularly prone to this sort of thing, but, to be fair, they have to carry much more about their person like landing nets, gaffs and fishing baskets, not to mention a rod, than the average sportsman. On the other hand, special belts from which dangle all manner of ironmongery from Swiss penknives to gadgets for taking flies out of fishes' mouths and funny hats with flies stuck all over them is going too far. Gentlemen never stick fishing flies in their hat except by accident.

It should also be remarked that gentlemen seldom wear anything but leather on their feet and most certainly not those green wellies with a little strap to tighten them at the top so beloved by the Sloane Rangers. This even applies to fishermen when wading. Here is an extract of some advice offered by that prince of sportsmen William Scrope at the end of the last century:

'… never go in deeper than the fifth button of your waistcoat; even this does not always agree with tender constitutions in frosty weather. As you are

likely not to take an estimate of cold in the excite-
ment of the sport, should you be of delicate tem-
perament, and wading in the month of February,
when it may chance to freeze very hard, pull down
your stockings and examine your legs. Should they
be black or even purple, it might, perhaps, be as
well to get on dry land; but if they are only rubi-
cund, you may continue to enjoy the water if it so
pleases you.'

Gentlemen are never afraid of getting their feet
wet nor, in fact, their persons. Mackintosh instead
of a tweed jacket is not greatly in favour and
certainly not those bulky affairs much favoured by
Americans, which make the wearer look like an
advertisement for Michelin tyres and scares the
wits out of any game bird, which will take the most
strenuous evasive action to avoid passing over his
head.

The modern, and fabulously expensive, carbon
fishing rods which are now all the rage might just
pass muster, though most gentlemen like to stick
to their old cane ones; however, the adoption of
the American style over-and-under shot guns, with
one barrel on top of the other will not win the
owner many envious glances at a good-class shoot.

"Guid God!"

The Gentleman and his Motor Car

It is no longer true to say that the gentleman lives in the age of the horse. There are indeed many gentlemen who, if invited to climb aboard a horse on one side would immediately fall off the other. However, the old attitudes linger on and this is nowhere more evident than in the gentleman's attitude to the motor car. Its sole purpose, in the eyes of the average gentleman, is as a means of getting from A to B with as little inconvenience as possible.

The one thing a gentleman's car is not is a status symbol to be lovingly taken out of the garage every Saturday morning to be washed and polished up to *concours d'elegance* standards in full view of the, hopefully, envious neighbours.

The function of the car as a means of establishing the social identity of the owner is an affliction from which non-gents suffer most horribly. At the lower end of the social scale this often takes the form of obscuring most of the front windscreen with names like Rodney or Daphne. Sometimes there are symbols like miniature football boots bouncing up and down and attached to the driver's mirror, matched by other dangly things on the back window like a fluffy doll or two or perhaps some witticism like 'Water-skiers do it standing up' or 'My other car is a BMW'.

This is something which does not mellow as the car owner grows wiser and wealthier. Quite the contrary. The social sherpa's motor car positively bristles with optional extras like telephones, cocktail cabinets and television sets, with affectations like smoked glass windows to emphasize to the passing peasantry that the occupants are persons of great importance and well worth looking at. The anti-show-off attitude of the gentleman makes it impossible for him to be seen in most of the status-symbol cars and particularly ones like the Rolls-Royce or things that can do 150 m.p.h. from a standing start in ten seconds. Thus this field is left clear for the likes of pop stars and the self-made tycoons of industry.

The most acceptable car for a gentleman is an estate car with a wired-off compartment at the back where he can lock away the younger children and his dogs for the duration of the journey. If he lives in the country he may well have several cars - one for going up and down hillsides so steep as to test the stamina of a mountain goat and which doubles, with bales of hay in the back, to serve as a make-shift grandstand at point-to-points and suchlike functions dear to the heart of the gentry.

Another car for the more travelled gentlemen is one for such excitements as going up and down to London. This sort of car is quite a different matter and he will, when buying it, study the form and consult his more knowledgeable friends, much in the same way as his forefathers would have done when contemplating the purchase of a potential Derby winner.

Nor, it must be said, is a gentleman, particularly of the younger generation, very much different from those of lesser social pretensions when it comes to getting behind the wheel. There is, however, a certain difference in attitude. Where the whoopee cowboy of the motorways, driving frantically, neatly pressed jacket swinging from a hook,

asserts his superiority by dodging in and out of the fast lane, lights flashing and horn blaring and marks his victories by a wild two-fingered stabbing of the air, the gentleman drives with just as much *élan* but not so much braggadocio. His attitude is simply one of 'Get out of my way or I'll ride right over you!' and he expects the opposition to do so. If on the other hand it is his mood to cruise along gently admiring the flowers by the wayside, he will happily do so in the fast lane and damn the more impatient as 'bloody road-hogs'.

The days are long past when a gentleman could afford to be intolerant if his wife wishes to have her own motor car, particularly if she is prepared to buy it out of her own money. Anything small and uncomfortable will do, providing he is not required to drive it.

Finally, if his car should contract some mechanical fault, either from neglect or natural causes, he would no more think of looking under the bonnet to diagnose the cause than he would attempt to operate on his horse without calling in the vet.

*"How she can smoke with a silver spoon and a plum in her
mouth, I can't think!"*

The Gentleman in the 1990's

The English Gentleman has certainly changed his spots but, behind the camouflage he has not really changed very much at all. Anyone who has taken this deeply researched work as seriously as it deserves to be taken should find little difficulty, after a suitable period of study, in equipping himself with the caste marks which will enable him to be recognized as a fellow-gentleman by those to the manner born. But what about the female of the species? In these days when Women's Lib. is into everything and women everywhere are chipping away industriously at the foundation stones of the male-dominated fortresses, do they in our new climate of society have an equal opportunity to promote themselves from the ranks so as to be recognized in their own right as English Ladies?

In fact, unfair though it may seem, should the new Boadiceas nurture any such ambitions in their marital bosoms, they will, I fear, find that they are tilting at windmills. The female of the species has always had it in her power to become acknowledged as a Lady in the time-honoured way of marrying a gentlemen established in Society and, thereafter, paying proper attention to acquiring the right caste marks.

There have, of course, always been ladies born with the metaphorical silver spoon in their mouths who have not always appreciated their good luck. Indeed, such is the perversity of human nature, there are many who have sought to disembarrass themselves of their inheritance at the earliest possible moment and seek solace in the arms of their

father's gamekeeper or in the hairy embrace of a
passing truck driver, thus losing the status to which
some of her less fortunate sisters under the skin
seek so ardently to aspire.

The main difficulty for those born below the salt
who attempt to go solo in improving their social
status is that they are apt to apply themselves to the
task with a fervour which amounts almost to para-
noia so that they quickly become figures of fun to
be made mock of by the disinterested observers of
their antics.

THE CHANGING SCENE

One of the factors which has contributed so much
to upsetting and confusing the social scene has
been the changing role in Society of the mistress.
In more settled days it was perfectly acceptable for
the English Gentleman to keep a mistress and,
indeed, in the case of French Gentlemen it was
almost *de rigeur*. The English Gentleman kept his
mistress in modest comfort in one of the smaller
types of house in Maida Vale or St John's Wood. He
would dally with her on those afternoons when he
was not otherwise engaged in racing or with a game
of cards in his club. The only condition laid down
by his wife was that he should be back home in time
to change for dinner, particularly if they were
entertaining guests.

The trouble in our new classless society is that
now, not only does every Tom, Dick and Harry feel
that he has a right to engage in extra-marital sexual
intercourse but the ladies whose affections are
engaged feel they have an equal right to a place
in the social sun as the lawfully wedded wife and
even, in extreme cases, may attempt to unseat her.

Thus the once-accepted gentlemanly practice of keeping a mistress has now been reduced to the more vulgar, and incidentally more dangerous, business of committing adultery which is quite a different thing. Mistress-keeping has now been abandoned by most gentleman except in some of the more remote corners of the shires. This leaves the field open to the wealthier type of middle-class tradesmen, commercial travellers and Members of Parliament to practise extra-marital sexual indulgence 1990s-style.

This shift in the social scene does not, of course, involve the working classes, it being generally agreed that sex is far too good for them and far above their station.

It is changes like these in the modern scene which makes the task of the social mountaineers, whether making a solo assault on the crest or as a mixed-doubles act, just that little bit more difficult. The climb is a slippery one with many an unseen crevasse into which the unwary climber may slip to the accompaniment of peals of well-bred laughter echoing from the icy peaks above.

Let us therefore look at one or two other aspects of the changing scene.

WHAT'S IN A NAME

The uniquely British practice of assuming hyphenated surnames has its origins in Victorian times and was originally adopted for a very practical reason, which was this. If the possessor of a fortune should die without issue or anyone to carry on the family name, it was often only on condition that the beneficiary should assume the family name of the benefactor. Thus a beneficiary, unwilling to

sacrifice his own patronym, got round the difficulty simply by adding the benefactor's name to his
own by means of a hyphen.

This had the effect of giving a hyphenated
surname a certain cachet to the world in general,
indicating, as it did, that the bearer would be likely
to be someone of substance in material terms and,
therefore, of social importance. It was not long
before some of the more socially ambitious families started to carry this to ridiculous lengths,
scattering hyphens around like confetti to establish their social prominence and finishing up with
names like Smythe-Brown-Piggott-Smythe.

This practice has grown into even greater dis-
pute in recent times, the hyphenating of surnames
having become the stock-in-trade of the confidence trickster or the socially pretentious to the
great embarrassment of older dynasties whose
names had originally been hyphenated for the
right reasons. It might also be mentioned here
that, for those born with a name like Smith or Jones
which they share with a great number of others, it
is perfectly proper, and indeed helpful to their
friends who want to look them up in the telephone
book to add a distinguishing description like
Lexington Smith or Forestier Jones, but these
additions should never be hyphenated.

There is also no reason why someone stuck with
a surname with which they are not happy, should
not change it. There was the case of one sensitive
soul who took a dislike to his name of Woodcock
and changed it to Oakhampton, a variation on a
theme which must appeal to the students of Cockney slang. There was also the socially ambitious
dark-skinned family who, not wishing entirely to

distance themselves from their ethnic origins, in deciding to adopt a hyphenated name, chose to call themselves the Goaley-Woges. Today it is generally considered affected to make variations of one's God-given name specially for reasons of social advancement. The upper classes, as in many other things, like to call a spade a spade.

SPEAKER PROPER

Many of the socially ambitious are apt to get into a fearful twist about whether or not they have an acceptable accent. In fact this does not count for a great deal. There are many gentlemen, brought up as they often are in the stable yard for example, who speak with very strange accents indeed. It is probably advisable for those who speak with the broader accents like Cockney, Geordie or Scouse to try to modify them if only to make themselves intelligible. Irish and Scottish accents, if not too exaggerated, can even be regarded as charming. If it is found to be too difficult to capture the English upper-class accent in full bray, do not try too hard. Unless it comes naturally to adopt the strangulated tones, with drawled vowels, which many feel to be a good imitation of the cut-glass accent attributed to the English upper classes, to try to do so is usually to court disaster.

U-SPEAK

Although Nancy Mitford went rather over the top with her jokey rabbiting-on about looking glasses and chimney pieces, there are certain words, or rather modes of expression, to which the upper classes are prone and which can be adopted to effect. There are, for example, certain words which can be traced back to nursery days and have stayed as common upper-class usage. For instance it is usual to call a vacuum-cleaner a 'Hoover' whatever the make of the machine might be. Abbreviations are not usually used. The refrigerator is not normally called a 'fridge' and more likely to be referred to by an early trade name like 'Frigidaire'. It is more likely for someone to ask 'Is there anything on television?' rather than on the 'telly' or 'TV'. A radio for any but the younger generation is normally called a wireless.

Certain terms of expression tend to have an old-fashioned ring about them. For the older generation the world is, by and large, divided into 'Good Eggs' and 'Bad Eggs'; there are still lots of 'cads' and 'rotters' around, not to mention the odd 'bad hat'. Girls are still referred to as 'gels' and there is no higher praise than to be called a 'capital gel', whilst one of more easy virtue might be dismissed as 'a little bit of snip-snap on the loose'. But on the whole it will be found rewarding to study the gentleman's usage of words and expressions rather than worry about the particular accent in which they pronounce them.

FILTHY LUCRE

Money is not a subject which should intrude into conversation between gentlemen, other perhaps that to bemoan the lack of it. It is an embarrassment for gentlemen who have a lot of the stuff and an equal embarrassment for those who are a bit short. Anyone who goes on about the quantity of his material goods or who by his actions, however well-intended and generous, seeks to boast of their extent is regarded as a vulgarian of the deepest dye and referred to as being 'filthy' or 'stinking' rich.

Any gentleman who has more than his fair share of the world's goods is described as being 'well-off' or 'comfortable'. It was Surtees' inimitable Jorrocks who described a really hard-up gentleman in the words: 'He was a gentleman who was generally spoken of having nothing a year, paid quarterly'. This would today be taken to mean someone who had had to cut his butler's salary in order to be able to send his son to Eton.

In this day and age it is, admittedly, increasingly difficult for the aspiring gentleman to assume the mantle of a gentleman without having a sufficiency of the necessary, but it is wiser and better to keep quiet about it.

PARTY MANNERS

In the eyes of many, to be a gentleman is synonymous with having good manners. 'He was always the perfect gentleman', as the tearful maiden traditionally wails when the cad who has done her wrong leaves her in the lurch. I suppose it to be generally true that gentlemen do normally take their hats off to ladies and stand up when they come into the room but to claim that a gentleman always has perfect manners is to come on a bit strong as anyone who has attended a coming-out party or a Hunt Ball will readily testify. This is usually put down to high spirits and is in sharp contrast to the brutish behaviour of persons of a lower social standing, nowadays often described as 'lager louts'. A gentleman of my acquaintance on being enquired of recently as to how a party he had attended had gone, replied that he had quite enjoyed it. 'Very few people said 'fuck' and nobody fell down' he explained reasonably enough, this probably being rather below par for the course.

One of the very first things the aspirant to social honours must learn is how to misbehave properly.

... AND FINALLY

One of the most important things of all to remember is that the true gentleman is at all times totally 'laid back'. Not for him the nervous sitting on the edge of the chair wondering which is the right knife and fork to use and trying to remember to use the butter knife when helping yourself to the butter. A truly relaxed gentleman will happily stir his tea with his fountain pen if no spoon happens to be provided or help himself to his own drink if his host is tardy in offering him one.

Oh, yes ... and for the very last word, let us defer once again to Jorrocks: 'No one knows how ungentlemanly he can look, until he sees himself in a shocking bad hat'.

A shocking bad hat